HOW DO WE MEASURE **?**

Speed

BLACKBIRCH PRESS

An imprint of Thomson Gale, a part of The Thomson Corporation

THOMSON
™
GALE

Detroit • New York • San Francisco • San Diego • New Haven, Conn. • Waterville, Maine • London • Munich

Consultant: Kimi Hosoume
Associate Director of GEMS (Great
    Explorations in Math and Science),
Director of PEACHES (Primary
    Explorations for Adults, Children,
    and Educators in Science),
Lawrence Hall of Science,
University of California,
Berkeley, California

For The Brown Reference Group plc
Text: Chris Woodford
Project Editor: Lesley Campbell-Wright
Designer: Lynne Ross
Picture Researcher: Susy Forbes
Illustrator: Darren Awuah
Managing Editor: Bridget Giles
Children's Publisher: Anne O'Daly
Production Director: Alastair Gourlay
Editorial Director: Lindsey Lowe

PHOTOGRAPHIC CREDITS
The Brown Reference Group plc: Edward Allwright 28, 29; **Corbis:** Alan Schein Photography
9t, Philip Bailey 17, Owen Franken 9b, Patrik Giardino 5, Reuters 10; **Corbis Saba:** Najlah
Feanny 11; **Empics:** Steve Mitchell 19t, Neal Simpson 19b; **Getty:** Roasnne Olson 15; **NASA:** 3,
7, 12, 22, 24, 27; **Photolibrary.com:** GMBH IFA-BILDERTEAM 4, OSF 13c,l&r; **Photos.com:** 1;
Rex Features: Heikki Saukkomaa 14; **Robert Hunt Picture Library:** 23; **SPL:** David A. Hardy 26,
NASA: 16; **Topham:** The Image Works/Larry Kolvoord 18; **U.S. Defense:** Eric A. Clement 20.

Front cover: **The Brown Reference Group plc:** Edward Allwright

LIBRARY OF CONGRESS CATALOGING-IN-PUBLICATION DATA

Woodford, Chris.
    Speed / by Chris Woodford.
        p. cm. — (How do we measure?)
    Includes bibliographical references and index.
    ISBN 1-4103-0370-5 (hardcover : alk. paper) — ISBN 1-4103-0526-0 (pbk. : alk.
paper)
    1. Speed—Measurement—Juvenile literature. I. Title II. Series: Woodford, Chris.
How do we measure?

    QC137.52.W66 2005
    531'.112—dc22

                                                                2004023442

Printed and bound in Thailand
10 9 8 7 6 5 4 3 2 1

Contents

What is speed?

Things are always moving in the world. Some things move fast. Cars and trucks, for example, whiz along on the freeway. Jet planes zoom overhead. Other things move more slowly. For example, earthworms and bugs crawl along in the soil underground. Even our fingernails are moving because they are growing very slowly!

Whether they go fast or slow, all moving things have speed. Speed is a measurement of how quickly or slowly something is moving.

Time and distance are related to speed

There is another way of thinking about speed. Speed is the time it takes for something to move a certain distance.

An airplane can fly from New York City to Los Angeles in less time than a car can drive there. The distance is about the same. So the airplane's speed is faster than the car's.

A speeding bullet cuts through a playing card. Bullets travel at such fast speeds that you cannot normally see them. This photograph has been taken using a special camera and film.

Speed and velocity

Velocity is the speed of an object that is moving in a particular direction. Two cars may have the same speed. But if you watch them drive in opposite directions, they have different velocities. If a race car goes around a curved track, it may keep the same speed.

But its velocity changes all the time because it is constantly turning in a different direction.

Even if these athletes are running at the same speed, they have different velocities because they are running in opposite directions.

Units of speed

Another way of looking at speed is to say it is the distance traveled divided by the time taken.

Speed = distance ÷ time

We can find a car's speed by measuring how far it goes and timing how long it takes.

Suppose a car drives 50 miles and takes one hour to do so. If it keeps traveling at this speed, it will cover 50 miles for each hour that it travels. That means its speed is 50 miles per hour, or 50 mph.

Speeds of fast-moving objects like cars, trucks, and trains are measured in miles per hour.

How fast is that?

A tortoise crawls very slowly, at around 0.2 mph.

Fingernails growing = 0.1 inch every two weeks
Tortoise = 0.2 mph
Person walking quickly = 4 mph
Hare running = 30 mph
Family car = 55 mph
Cheetah running = 70 mph
Race car = 150 mph
Jumbo Jet = 500 mph
Flying bullet = 1,750 mph
Fastest military airplane = 2,000 mph
Space rocket leaving Earth = 25,000 mph

Miles per hour are called units of speed. A unit is something that tells us how big a measurement is—50 miles per hour is a very different speed from 50 inches per hour. The number is the same, but the units are different.

Cars, airplanes, and even space rockets measure their speeds in miles per hour. Things that move more slowly have their speeds measured in other ways. A snail cannot crawl even one mile in an hour. Its speed is measured in inches per minute.

A space shuttle takes off. When a rocket is launched, it travels away from Earth at very fast speeds— around 25,000 miles per hour.

Metric speeds

To measure speed, we have to measure both distance and time. Distance can be measured with two different kinds of units. One kind is imperial units such as miles, feet, yards, or inches. These units are sometimes called customary units. If imperial units are used to to measure distance, the speed measured is also imperial. Imperial measurements of speed include miles per hour and feet per second.

Distance is also measured with metric units such as kilometers (km), meters (m), and centimeters (cm). Metric units are

Changing speeds — imperial to metric and back again

Sometimes speeds are written in imperial units and at other times, they are written in metric units.

Imperial to metric
1 mile per hour (mph) is the same as 1.6 kilometers per hour (km/h)
1 foot per second is the same as 30 centimeters per second
1 mile per hour is the same as 0.4 meters per second

Metric to imperial
1 kilometer per hour is the same as 0.6 miles per hour
1 meter per second is the same as 3 feet 3 inches per second

This speedometer (above) is a device found in cars, trucks, and bikes. It measures speed in both imperial units (the outer circle of numbers) and metric units (inner numbers).

part of the metric system. The metric system is based on the meter, a distance of around 39 inches. If distance is measured in metric units, the measurement of speed is also in metric units. Metric measurements of speed include meters per second and kilometers per second.

Fast speeds

Cars, airplanes, and sprint runners go very fast. But their speed can still be measured. Whether things go fast or slow, their speed is always the distance traveled divided by the time it takes.

Speed = distance ÷ time

We cannot tell how fast a runner is going just by looking. But we can time how long the runner takes to run a distance of 100 yards or 100 meters. That will tell us the runner's speed.

One way to measure the speed of a very fast airplane is to time how long it takes to fly a very long distance. It takes a jet airplane about six hours to fly from New York

A photo finish of a 400-meter race at the Sydney Olympics in 2000 shows who has run fastest.

Laser guns

This policeman is aiming a laser gun at a passing car to find out how fast it is traveling. The gun's computer figures out the speed and displays it.

City to Los Angeles. Measured in a straight line, the distance between these two cities is about 2,400 miles. So the airplane must fly at a speed of 2,400 miles divided by 6 hours, or 400 mph.

Police officers can tell if someone is driving too fast by using a special gun that fires an invisible laser beam. The laser beam hits the car and bounces back into the gun.

The car's speed changes the way the laser beam travels. A computer in the gun detects this change and figures out how fast the car is going.

Slow motion

Sometimes things move so fast that we cannot see them. And sometimes we cannot notice speed because it happens too slowly. Many things in nature are very slow. Plants are moving because they are always growing. But most grow so slowly that we cannot see them. It can take hundreds of years for a tree to grow, for example. So the speed at which a tree grows is only a few inches every year.

The San Andreas fault line runs over 800 miles (1,300 km) along the Pacific coast of North America. Its slow movement has caused some of the world's biggest earthquakes.

Some changes happen even more slowly. Earthquakes happen around cracks in the earth called fault lines. Fault lines move at a speed of perhaps just a quarter inch per year. That does not sound like much. But every so often this slow movement can lead to a huge earthquake, killing many people and causing a lot of damage.

Speeding up

In this first picture, only one flower bud has begun to open.

A little later, several more buds have slowly flowered.

After an even longer time, nearly all of the buds have opened.

One way we can see invisible speeds is to make them happen more quickly. We could leave a movie camera running for a day or a week so it films a flower opening. Then we could speed up the movie so the flower opens in a few seconds. This trick is called time-lapse photography. Many TV nature programs use it.

Spinning around

Something that moves without getting anywhere must be moving in a circle. Moving in a circle is called rotating, or revolving. Lots of things move like this. For example, machines in a factory can rotate at very high speeds, but they never get anywhere.

Even if things rotate, their speed can still be measured. Speed is the distance traveled in a certain time. If something moves in a circle, it does not travel any distance. But that does not mean its speed is zero. We need a special way of measuring speed for something that rotates.

This man is taking part in a sport called hammer throwing. To make the hammer travel farther, he spins around very fast before releasing it.

People on this merry-go-round revolve around and around. They do not travel anywhere but they are still moving at speed.

Spinning Earth

The universe is like a gigantic clockwork machine. All the planets are constantly rotating around themselves and around the Sun. It takes a year for Earth to move once around the Sun. So Earth's speed is one rotation per year. Earth also spins as it moves around the Sun. It takes one day for Earth to rotate once. So Earth's spinning speed is one rotation per day.

We have to measure how often the item turns around in a certain amount of time. Each time it turns around is called one rotation, or revolution. If a spinning top turns around 10 times in 1 minute, we say its speed is 10 revolutions per minute, or 10 rpm. An engine might turn around at hundreds or thousands of rpm.

Speeding up and slowing down

Things do not always travel at the same speed. Sometimes they speed up and sometimes they slow down. A car cannot reach its top speed right away. If it starts from being parked, the car will take some time to go as fast as it can.

If the driver steps on the gas, the car goes faster and faster, and its speed increases.

This series of photographs shows what happens when someone experiences a very rapid acceleration strapped into a special rocket sled.

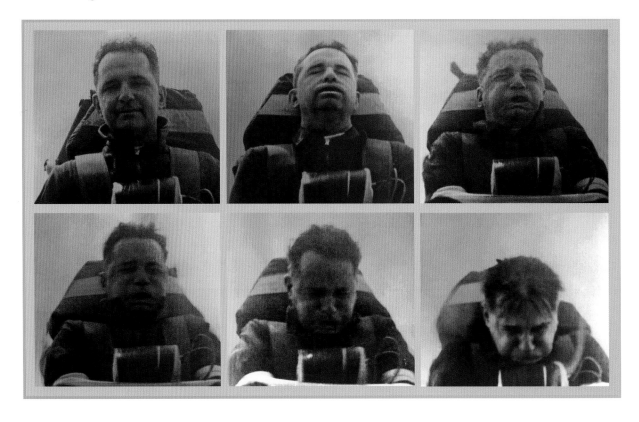

Measuring acceleration

A race car driver accelerates hard at the start of a race to make the car travel as fast as possible.

When something's speed increases, it is called acceleration. When something's speed slows down, or decreases, it is called deceleration.

Acceleration is how fast something's speed increases. If a car or truck accelerates quickly, for example, its speed also changes quickly. If it accelerates slowly, it takes longer for the car to reach its top speed.

Suppose a car is driving along at 25 mph. The driver steps on the gas for 10 seconds and the car speeds up to 55 mph. We can measure the acceleration in the following way. First, we need to know how much the speed has changed. It is 55 mph minus 25 mph, or 30 mph. The change in speed took 10 seconds to happen. So the acceleration is 30 mph in 10 seconds.

Speed on land

There are all sorts of reasons why people need to measure speed. For example, car drivers need to know how fast they are going so they drive safely and keep below the speed limit. All cars are fitted with gauges on the dashboard called speedometers. They measure the car's speed and display it in mph and kph. A speedometer works by counting how quickly the car's wheels turn around.

People also measure speed during races. Races usually take place over a set distance, such as 100 yards or 100 meters. We can tell how fast people are going by timing how long they take to run a certain distance. Accurate stopwatches are used to measure the time exactly.

Children running in a cross-country event run the distance in a certain time, so their speed can be calculated.

If someone runs 100 yards in 15 seconds, his or her speed is 100 divided by 15, or 6.7 yards per second.

$$100 \div 15 = 6.7 \text{ yards per second}$$

This finishing-line camera (right) photographs the winner of the race.

Photo finish

Some races happen very fast. It can be hard to tell who won or how fast they were going. Most racetracks have a camera at the finish line. As the runners cross the line, the camera takes a series of photographs. The picture shows who won the race and how fast they were running. Photo finishes are also used in horse races.

These women are running side by side. If they crossed the finish line together, it would be hard to figure out who had won and at what speed without using a camera.

Speed at sea

It is much harder to measure distance at sea than on land. The tumbling waves and the lack of landmarks can make it hard for a ship to know how far it has gone. That makes it harder to measure speed at sea.

In olden times, people measured the speed of a ship using a special rope. The rope had knots tied in it at equal distances. Sailors would drop the rope off the stern (back) of the ship and see how long it took to unravel. The faster the ship went, the faster the knotted

Modern ships like this American navy ship have lots of gauges and other instruments to calculate their speed and distance of travel.

rope fell into the sea. The ship's speed would be measured as so many knots per hour.

Knots are still used to measure the speed of ships today, although ships now have speedometers much like cars. A knot is equal to just over 1.1 miles per hour (1.8 km per hour). So a ship that sails at a speed of 20 knots is going at 22 mph (35 km per hour).

Making waves

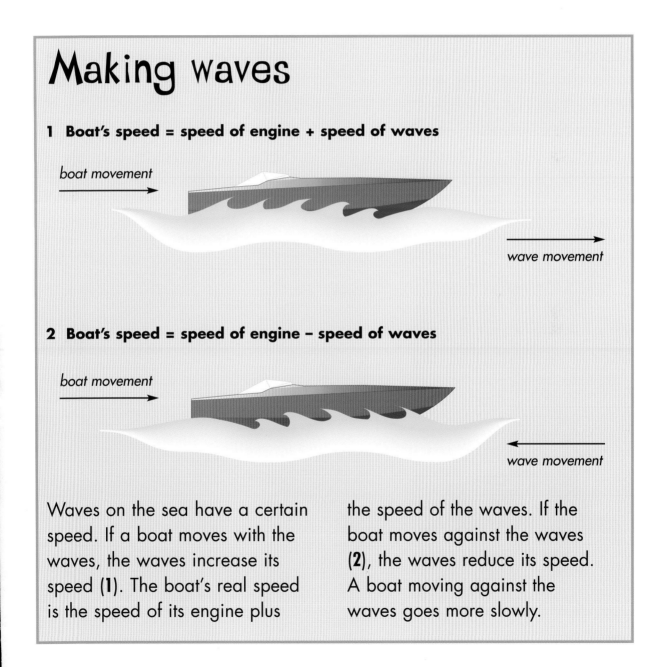

1 Boat's speed = speed of engine + speed of waves

boat movement

wave movement

2 Boat's speed = speed of engine – speed of waves

boat movement

wave movement

Waves on the sea have a certain speed. If a boat moves with the waves, the waves increase its speed (**1**). The boat's real speed is the speed of its engine plus the speed of the waves. If the boat moves against the waves (**2**), the waves reduce its speed. A boat moving against the waves goes more slowly.

Speed in the air

Airplanes are the fastest things most people ever see. When the Wright brothers made the first working airplane in 1903, it had a top speed of 30 mph (48 km/h). Airplane designers now try to make planes that will fly at 7,200 mph (11,500 km/h). That speed is 240 times faster than the Wright brothers ever flew!

Air makes it difficult for planes to fly fast. Air pushes against a plane, which makes the plane slow down. That is called air resistance. Air resistance can be a big problem when planes fly near the speed of sound, which is about 660 mph (1,056 km/h). As planes fly at this speed, they make a very load roaring noise called a sonic boom.

This is an artist's drawing of NASA's Hyper-X43A hypersonic plane. It flies without a pilot at seven to ten times the speed of sound.

The first airplane was designed and built by Orville and Wilbur Wright more than 100 years ago.

Planes that fly faster than the speed of sound are supersonic. They have to be specially shaped to fly faster than sound. They have very sleek noses and wings to cut through the air. Hypersonic planes can fly at least five times faster than sound, or about 3,300 mph (5,280 km/h). The space shuttle is a hypersonic plane.

World trip

In 1977 a PanAm "Jumbo Jet" set a world speed record for flying around Earth. It went around the entire globe and over both the North and South poles. The plane traveled a total distance of 26,383 miles (42,213 km) in just 54 hours and 7 minutes. The plane's average speed was nearly 500 mph (800 km/h)!

Speed in space

Space is a vast place of enormous distances and times that seem to go on forever. And it is getting bigger all the time. In 1929 U.S. astronomer Edwin Hubble (1889–1953) found that the universe is expanding, or increasing in size. He saw that the universe is like a balloon that is slowly being blown up. Hubble wanted to find out how fast the universe was expanding. He had to figure out how he could measure a speed like that.

As the universe expands, stars and galaxies move away from Earth. That changes the way they shine their light toward Earth, and the way we see

Stars and galaxies moving away from Earth show redshift, or shine redder, as the universe expands.

that light. If galaxies are moving away, they seem to shine a little redder. That is called redshift. Hubble measured how fast galaxies are moving by measuring how red they looked. That told him how fast the universe is expanding.

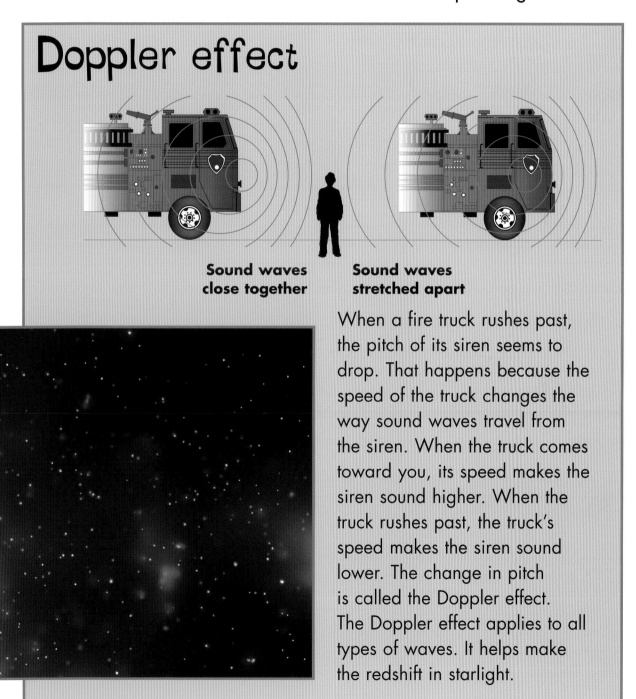

Doppler effect

Sound waves close together

Sound waves stretched apart

When a fire truck rushes past, the pitch of its siren seems to drop. That happens because the speed of the truck changes the way sound waves travel from the siren. When the truck comes toward you, its speed makes the siren sound higher. When the truck rushes past, the truck's speed makes the siren sound lower. The change in pitch is called the Doppler effect. The Doppler effect applies to all types of waves. It helps make the redshift in starlight.

Speed of light

Light travels at the incredible speed of 186,291 miles (298,066 km) per second. Nothing can go faster than that. The speed of light is like universe's speed limit. It took scientists many years to measure the speed of light.

Galileo's experiment

In the 17th century, a famous Italian scientist named Galileo Galilei (1564–1642) tried to measure the speed of light. He did this by flashing a lantern to a friend some distance away. But he found light travels too fast to measure its speed like that.

A drawing of a spaceship. Spaceships travel very fast, but never as fast as the speed of light.

Dead stars

Some of the stars we can see are no longer really there. They stopped shining millions of years ago. But they are so far away that the light they sent out is still traveling toward Earth. Light travels very fast. But if a light beam has to travel from one side of the universe to the other, it can still take millions of years for it to reach Earth.

In the 1850s, a Frenchman named Armand Fizeau (1819–1896) became the first person to measure the speed of light. He used a spinning wheel to make a light beam travel a very long way. Fizeau timed the light beam and that gave him a measurement for the speed of light.

When you look at the sky at night, you will see the light from millions of shining stars. Some of these stars died and stopped sending out light many millions of years ago. But starlight must travel a great distance so it takes a very long time to reach Earth. So although some stars no longer exist, we can still see their light.

Measure your speed

1 Make a mark on the ground with the chalk. Now measure out a distance of 100 yards or 100 feet, in a straight line, from the chalk mark. Make another mark on the ground at the end of the distance.

You will need:
- A ruler or tape measure
- A clock or watch with a second hand or a stopwatch
- A piece of chalk
- A long, straight sidewalk or piece of land
- A friend to help you

2 Walk from one chalk line to the other. Ask your friend to time how long that takes.

3 Figure out your speed. You do this by dividing the distance you walked by the time it took. So if you walked 100 yards in 30 seconds, your speed is $100 \div 30 = 3.3$ yards per second.

4 Now try running the distance between the two chalk marks. Ask your friend to time how long it takes. The time should be much less than when you walked. Figure out your speed in the same way. How much faster did you run?

5 Change places with your friend. Ask him or her to walk and run the distance, just as you did, and write down the times.

6 Figure out his or her walking and running speeds. Which of you walks the fastest? Which of you runs fastest?

Glossary

acceleration A change in speed that makes something go faster.

centimeter A small metric unit of measurement equal to one meter divided by 100.

customary unit Another term for an imperial unit.

deceleration A change in speed that makes something go slower.

Doppler effect The way speed changes the observed light or sound of a moving object.

hypersonic A speed that is at least five times faster than the speed of sound.

imperial A traditional measurement. Miles, feet, and inches, are imperial units of measure.

kilometers per hour A metric measurement of speed. There are 1,000 meters in a kilometer.

knot A measurement of speed at sea (1 knot equals 1.1 miles per hour).

kph A short way of writing kilometers per hour.

measurement A way of finding out how tall, long, big, or fast something is.

meter A metric measurement equal to about 3.3 feet.

metric system A modern system of measurements based on the meter.

miles per hour An imperial measurement of speed.

mph A short way of writing miles per hour.

motion Another way of describing movement.

redshift The way distant stars seem redder because they are moving away.

revolution One complete turn of a spinning object.

rotation One complete turn of a spinning object.

speedometer A gauge that measures speed in a car, truck, or bike.

unit The part of a measurement that tells us how big or small it is: inches, feet, and miles, for example.

supersonic A speed that is faster than the speed of sound.

velocity A speed measured in a certain direction.

Find out more _____

Books

Alan Rubin, *Fast and Faster*. Chatham, MA: Yellow Umbrella, 2003.

Ian Graham, *The Best Book of Speed Machines*. Boston: Kingfisher/Houghton Mifflin, 2002.

Laura Driscoll and Page Eastburn O'Rourke, *Slow Down, Sara*. New York: Kane Press, 2003.

Robert E. Wells, *What's Faster Than a Speeding Cheetah?* Morton Grove, IL: Albert Whitman, 1997.

Robert Gardner, *Split-Second Science Projects With Speed: How Fast Does It Go?* Berkeley Height, N.J.: Enslow, 2003.

Web sites

Astronomy for Kids: Redshift
Learn more about redshift and how it happens
www.dustbunny.com/afk/
    skywonders/redshift/

Faster than Sound
Breaking the sound barrier
www.pbs.org/wgbh/nova/barrier/

Index